MEAT
LONDON
AN INSIDER'S GUIDE

**black dog
publishing**
london uk

MENU

RESTAURANTS & PUBS

MENU

RESTAURANTS & PUBS

MENU

STREET FOOD

MENU

BUTCHERS

PROLOGUE

Meat London: An Insider's Guide isn't meant to be a comprehensive restaurant guide. Nor is it meant to be regular tourist handbook. Rather, it has been compiled as a select and inclusive insight into some of the more acclaimed, on-trend and interesting foodie institutions in the capital. Inevitably, given the current good health of London's food scene, we could have added consistently to the list throughout the book's production. This not being tenable, the establishments focused on present something more of a delicious snapshot in time. And as such, *Meat London: An Insider's Guide* incorporates both edgy upstarts and long standing gastro favourites, established names and more obscure game changers all sharing an obsession with good meat.

This contemporary 'snapshot' will highlight both positive and unfortunate truths in our eating and shopping habits. Whilst it is certain that the integrity and diversity in the gastronome underground will continue to grow, it is important to note that many of these businesses—and I'm thinking here particularly of a number of the butchers' shops detailed in the book—are under serious threat of closure due to the increasing homogenisation of our high streets and shopping tastes. Supporting these long-running, valuable enterprises is a necessary factor in keeping our foodie traditions alive. The proprietors of these provide a wealth of informed expertise and values that a chain supermarket simply cannot—or will not—and it would be a tragedy to lose this.

In addition to these more traditional institutions, London has also been witness to an explosively ascendant street food scene in recent years. Moveable feasts are now ubiquitous around the capital, with regular spots at gastro-hubs such as Broadway Market in Hackney, Brockley Market, Leather Lane near Farringdon, North Cross Road in Dulwich, Brick Lane, Whitecross Market in Clerkenwell and Eat St in King's Cross. That Petra Barran, the Eat St collective's founder and driving force, was named one of the "Ten people who changed the world" by *The Independent* in 2011 is indicative of how far the movement has come. The growth of London's taste for independent street food start-ups has been astounding, and passionate individuals initiate new ventures almost weekly.

Increasingly, a critical conception of 'good food' directly correlates with good practises. Thus, we've also tried to highlight which individuals, eateries and butchers are maintaining an explicit commitment to regionality, seasonality, efforts in reducing food miles and increasing—or rather, upping an exposure of—trends in 'nose-to-tail' eating. Of course, these elements have long been prevalent in London—just perhaps not as widely discussed or considered as important in the media as they are now. Individuals like Fergus Henderson and Trevor Gulliver of St John, for example, have barely changed their remit in the past decade and a half: a dedication to good food by way of good ethics. That so many people have found inspiration in this, taken up a similar mantel and mindset and provided us with so much to get excited about is nothing but commendable.

Thomas Howells

INTRODUCTION

"Plates of meat", the old cockney rhyming slang for "feet", is a phrase seldom heard these days, though it's one that you, the reader and visitor to our capital, may well find yourself reaching to use after padding around this great city. But if, along the way, you've picked up this fine book, then plates of meat must be what you're looking for in a very literal sense.

AND YOU HAVE CHOSEN WISELY

London has long enjoyed a reputation for good shopping and eating and in the past decade or so that reputation has only swelled, placing it alongside New York and Paris as one of the most exciting cities in which to dine.

I worked for more than a decade at the London restaurant that many consider, perhaps more than any other has influenced how chefs prepare meat and diners eat it.

Fergus Henderson's St John in Smithfield applied a principle of 'nose-to-tail' eating; by which every part of the animal was game for the plate—in short that it bordered on impolite to slaughter an animal, fowl or fish and not consider how all of it might be put to good and delicious use in the kitchen.

Fergus would blush to be told he had such influence, but that credo filtered out through alumni opening their own restaurants (Jonathon Jones at The Anchor & Hope in Waterloo, Tom Pemberton at Hereford Road in West London) and further still by others adopting the code. Today, quality of meat and the flavour to be mined from lesser used cuts and rare breeds has become of paramount importance.

MEAT IS NOW VERY MUCH THE STAR

At the time of writing we're living through the big dip, a recession that has seen the global economy wither precariously. But as with previous slumps, rents go down, otherwise forgotten neighbourhoods rise, enterprising and creative types see and grasp opportunity and ideas blossom and thrive—and nowhere else in London will you see this flourish as healthily than in its food scene.

Food lovers and culinary tweeters feverishly book for word-of-mouth led one offs in 'greasy spoon' cafes that transform at night into temples to the perfect Spaghetti Bolognese or Vongole.

Forgotten pub dining rooms play host to the sort of burger joints John Travolta would take Uma Thurman to in *Pulp Fiction* and enthused amateurs open their living rooms up to strangers as the supper club bug takes an ever tighter hold.

Those without a kitchen and dining room of their own, meanwhile, have made the streets their restaurant.

Food wagons such as Pitt Cue Co. parked up underneath Hungerford Bridge and served pulled pork so good some said it gave the Americas a run for its money. Eager trenchermen (and women) joined winding queues for hotdogs of the highest order from Big Apple Hot Dogs in Old Street.

But so much choice can be dizzying. The uninformed visitor in search of sustenance may easily stumble into the tourist trap, the mundane chain restaurant or meal deal limbo, missing the chance to feast on the excellent produce cooked with skill by the enthused chef.

Your A–Z map won't lead you to the brawn Ed Wilson serves at Brawn in the East, nor to the sliders and appetite-sharpening cocktails served by tattooed waiters at Spuntino and its West End siblings.

And that Dorling Kindersley London pocketbook won't help you find Tom Barton's exquisite burgers at Honest Burgers in the regenerated Brixton Village, or Bob Dove's fine butcher's shop in Battersea.

No. The committed meat fan needs a bespoke, proper guide to the very best of London's butchers, street food vendors and dining rooms, and you, fortunate traveller, are clasping the very thing right now!

Keep *Meat London: An Insider's Guide* to hand as you pad the flagstones and hop on and off the Routemaster buses and tubes and plan wisely—eat a moderate breakfast (though if you want to get your meat quota out of the way early, Hawksmoor is a good place to start the day).

So, welcome to our great city of eating. Easy on the ketchup, hold the mayo and don't forget the mustard.

Thomas Blythe

Corner Room

THE ANCHOR & HOPE

The Anchor & Hope
36 The Cut
SE1 8LP

020 7928 9898

Aside from The Eagle, The Anchor & Hope is perhaps the best-known and longest standing gastropub in London. Rob Shaw and Jonathon Jones met whilst working at St John, and were friends with Eagle chef Harry Lester. With backing from Michael Belben—The Eagle's owner—and following a successful pop-up 'lunch club' (as such ventures were then known) they opened The Anchor & Hope in 2003. Shaw took up front of house duties, whilst Jones and Lester manned the kitchen.

Rob Shaw has emphatically stated that the original ethos behind The Anchor & Hope was to keep "its pub identity whilst serving fantastic food and brilliant drinks", something they have maintained successfully if continuing critical praise is to be believed. The food is seasonal and ingredient-led with a focus on offal and game, as it has been from the beginning. Further, carcasses are bought whole and are butchered in-house; the entire animal is used in the pub's rustic, gutsy cooking. As at Shaw's and Jones' other restaurants—Great Queen Street, The Canton Arms, and the excellent Magdalen Arms in Oxford—sharing dishes are as much a draw as those for one; these could include a rib of beef for two, a neck or shoulder of lamb for three or five(ish), or even a whole shin of beef cooked overnight for ten.

BISTROT BRUNO LOUBET

Bistrot Bruno Loubet
St John's Square
86–88 Clerkenwell Road
EC1M 5RJ

020 7324 4455
www.bistrotbrunoloubet.com

Bruno Loubet is perhaps the most famous chef you might never have heard of. He worked under Pierre Koffman at La Tante Claire (and much later at the chef's pop-up venture at Selfridges in 2009) and was Head Chef at Le Manoir aux Quat' Saisons in Oxfordshire, before opening his own lauded London establishments Bistro Bruno and L'Odean in the mid-1990s. After eight successful years in Australia, Loubet returned to London to open the eponymous Bistrot in the slick confines of Clerkenwell's Zetter Townhouse in 2010.

The critical and popular buzz around his return —at first anticipant, then emphatically proven—was palpable; Bistrot Bruno Loubet has ended up being one of the most conspicuously loved London eateries in recent memory.

This is wholly down to the Bistrot's affordability and warm aesthetic, and Loubet's genuinely exciting reinterpretation and appropriation of traditional French cooking. Dishes such as "Roasted rump of lamb, broad bean ratatouille and pumpkin seed pesto", "Braised beef Indochine, mango and herb salad" and "Boned and rolled rabbit saddle, crushed roasted pumpkin, wild garlic and peas" are elegantly presented and richly complex. Loubet's signature, though, is the much-written about seasonal "Hare Royale", comprising a rich disc of diced hare meat —itself one of the heavier, more muskily gamey of meats—and foie gras, with wild mushrooms, pureed potato and an unctuous, heavily reduced sauce.

BISTROT
BRUNO LOUBET

7.00
7.50
7.50
8.50
8.00
8.50
8.50
7.50

STARTERS

Watercress soup with soft poached egg
Sautéed padron peppers, organic ricotta, Romesco sauce
Sardine escabèche and piquillo pepper mousse
Guinea fowl boudin blanc, petit pois à la Française
...ravioli, rocket salad, fried breadcrumbs and Parmesan
...and meatballs, royale de champignon sauvage
... Niçoise style
... smoked cod roe, apple compote, seaweed oil

butter

BOCCA DI LUPO

Bocca Di Lupo
12 Archer Street
W1D 7BB

020 7734 2223
www.boccadilupo.com

Chef Jacob Kennedy—previously of Moro—and partner Victor Hugo could be considered partly responsible for the popularity of the burgeoning 'small plates' trend in London over the past few years. Their flagship establishment Bocca Di Lupo opened in 2008, serving unpretentious, gutsy regional Italian food to an in-the-know Soho crowd. The restaurant has been consistently praised since; notably, Kennedy's constantly (sometimes twice-daily) changing menus explicitly reference the regional provenance of his authentic dishes, which have included such rustic plates and delicacies as "Veal tongue, peara [a bread and bone marrow polenta] home-candied mostarda and salsa verde" from Verona; Calabrian orecchiette with 'nduja; Venetian foie gras and pork sausages known as "luganega", which are flavoured with nutmeg, cinnamon and cloves; skewers of lamb's sweetbreads and artichokes from Lazio; and, now a touch infamously, an edgily heavy Sicilian dish of spleen and lung simmered in lard and served with focaccia bread and smoke ricotta. Dishes can be ordered in large or small portions—hence the restaurant's contribution to the aforementioned zeitgeist—and in addition, tiny "Fritti Romani"—such as outstanding veal and pork stuffed olives—arrive individually priced.

The restaurant's interior aesthetic smacks of moneyed, low-key formality; the pastel walls and inoffensive paintings feel slightly incongruous given the cooking, but the visible kitchen behind the bar lends a buzzing atmosphere and the exterior red brick facade and chunky typeface is unusual and attractive.

BRAWN

Brawn
49 Columbia Road
E2 7RG

020 7729 5692
www.brawn.co

Opened in 2010 as the hip little sister to the excellent Terroirs wine bar in Charing Cross, Brawn—as one might imagine given the name—is a robustly meaty affair, with a focus on offal and French-style dishes, as well as natural wines sourced from small, biodynamic and organic growers and producers.

Signature staples such as the titular pig's head terrine and pork rillettes—both from the section of the menu simply entitled "Pig"—are simple, rustic dishes, both rich enough to warrant understating their voguey 'small dish' portions.

The menu flits between "Taste Tickler"'s, the aforementioned "Pig", "Plancha", "Hot" and "Puddings and Cheese". Fish and a few vegetarian plates feature—at least on our visit, though the menu changes daily according to seasonality and market availability—but meat is the main deal here. "Hand chopped Tuscan style beef"—a simplified tartare devised from a staff trip to northern Italy with beef substituted in for the traditional raw pork—is as basic as dishes come and excellently carnivorous. A giant caillette faggot was supremely herby, whilst a brawn and trotter combination of Tamworth Pig, served with bitter chicory and a heavy gribiche sauce, was an unctuous treat and the highpoint from a consistently excellent kitchen.

BUEN AYRE

Buen Ayre
50 Broadway Market
E8 4QJ

020 7275 9900
www.buenayre.co.uk

John Rattagan's much-loved Argentine parrilla Buen Ayre was the first of its kind in the UK. After leaving Argentina at the age of 25 to study in London, Rattagan took up a grill position at the Duke of Edinburgh pub in Brixton—allegedly working under the guise of spuriously romantic alter-ego Cacho Gómez—before setting up his flagship restaurant on Hackney's Broadway Market. Despite a professed lack of prior experience in the restaurant business, his dedication to providing London with a conspicuously missing Argentine grill—the Gaucho chain, he emphatically states, does not count—has been a great success, consistently lauded in the press and highly regarded by gastronomes across the capital.

Unsurprisingly, beef is the main draw at Buen Ayre, and the restaurant's signature dish is its leviathan Deluxe Grill; it consists of two massive steaks—a rib eye and a sirloin, both sourced from Argentina—two Argentine-style sausages (made in England to a specific recipe devised by Rattagan), black pudding and a slice of melted provolone cheese, along with sundries such as the Argentine sauce chimichurri, traditionally served with grilled meats and consisting of a basic mix of chopped parsley, crushed garlic, olive oil, oregano and vinegar.

The restaurant's wine list is overwhelmingly Argentinian—no great surprise and definitely a plus given the country's infamously consistent wine industry—and the aesthetic is carried through to Buen Ayre's decoration, with retro Argentine ephemera and imagery dotted around the warm, intimate dining room.

THE BULL & LAST

The Bull & Last
168 Highgate Road
NW5 1QS

020 7267 3641
www.thebullandlast.com

Idyllically located on the Parliament Hill side of Hampstead Heath, The Bull & Last opened in 2008 at first to quiet acceptance—gastropubs are not a rare sight in this moneyed area of north London— and then rapturous fanfare as the gushing reviews rolled in. The pub itself is split into a crowded downstairs bar-cum-eatery, with the upstairs a more straightforwardly refined dining room, both decorated with charmingly sizeable taxidermy (moose, bulls and bibbed-up foxes feature) and English country ephemera appropriate to their Grade II listed surroundings. Furniture is mismatching and recovered, lending a warm, rural cosiness to proceedings.

The food is English and seasonal, complemented by the range of changing and local London real ales on tap. The Bull's scotch eggs—infamous even before the inescapable trend for gourmet versions of the snack became ubiquitous around town—and Sunday roasts—once again rated the best in the capital, according to *Time Out*—are perennial critical darlings, but the menu is consistently excellent; rosemary flecked sausage rolls were sizeable, the giant charcuterie board—encompassing brawn, smoked duck, terrine, a very fine parfait, rillettes, remoulade, cornichons and sourdough—was exemplary, and bettered only by a faultless stuffed leg of guinea fowl with olives and hazelnut puree.

Seasonality and provenance is also at the fore of the Bull's priorities; occasionally seen on chalkboards around the pub, there is also a full list on their website, with most produce being sourced within London, the south of England and Wales.

THE CANTON ARMS

The Canton Arms
177 South Lambeth Road
SW8 1XP

020 7582 8710
www.cantonarms.com

A former local boozer—ostensibly still the case, save for the dining room behind the period horseshoe bar—and reformed hive of (alleged) firearms trading, The Canton Arms is probably the most appealing place to eat in Stockwell. Its current incarnation was brought to life by Trish Hilferty—previously of The Eagle in Farringdon—and the reliable minds behind The Anchor & Hope and Great Queen Street. Like at those institutions, the menu maintains an uncomplicated, gutsy dedication to hefty meaty flavours.

The dining room is a warm space of bare, shared tables, menu specials scrawled on blackboards and shelves of piled heavy iron pots and home-made pickles, syrups and jams. The food itself is robust, to say the least. Heavy on game and unusual cuts —inevitable given its founder's professional heritage —one can expect to see dishes such as wood pigeon, Hampshire pork with polenta and share-size cuts of onglet with aioli on the efficiently short menu. Particularly good are the giant blackboard dishes for full tables of diners; a remarkably tender stewed lamb neck arrived in a scorching Le Creuset casserole straight from the oven, with a leviathan tray of potato dauphinoise following.

A mention must go to the pub's idiosyncratic bar snacks, specifically the toasted sandwiches filled with haggis—a genius use of the spicy, earthy mince—and foie gras, the latter of which was perhapsalittle overbearing in its rich fattiness, but gluttonously delicious all the same, and an agreeable accompaniment to the bar's permanent and guest ales.

Corner Room
Town Hall Hotel
Patriot Square
E2 9NF

No phone
www.townhallhotel.com/
corner_room

Nuno Mendes' Viajante—a haven to trends in fiddly, microscopic gastronomy—received fairly divisive reviews on opening due to the highfalutin, sometimes middlingly experimental nature of its fare. Corner Room is situated, like Viajante, in Bethnal Green's plush and modern Town Hall Hotel, though inconspicuously located in a tiny upstairs space. This venture is purely à la carte, serving small, beautifully presented and almost laughably reasonable dishes compared to the eye watering prices downstairs.

The menu is basic in its listing of each of a dish's individual ingredients, though the plates themselves arrive as tiny works of art. Corner Room's remit is not purely meaty—dishes such as "Confit salmon with beetroot and horseradish", and a deconstructed "Dark chocolate with peanut butter ice cream" prove equally as intriguing—though it is signature plates such as the "Ibérico pork plumas and Portuguese bread pudding" and "Lamb with cereals and roast garlic" which really bring Mendes' innovative approach to cooking to the fore. The former—served rare, and perfectly complemented by the intense umami hit of the bread "pudding", which is actually a small pile of breadcrumbs intensely infused with herbs, tomato and chorizo oil—has been particularly lauded.

THE DELI WEST ONE

The Deli West One
51 Blandford Street
W1U 7JH

020 7224 4033
www.thedelilondon.com

Marylebone's The Deli West One is one of London's best-regarded authentic Jewish delis. It was opened in November 2011, by four men—enigmatically un-named—bought together by a collective desire to bring strictly Kosher, New York-style deli fare to the capital; specifically, they state, two "longed for a proper [beef] hotdog", "a third was on a quest for succulent tongue" and the fourth was searching for a chicken soup comparable to that made by his mother.

The continuing critical acclaim would suggest that they've been successful in their intentions. Their Kosher credentials, for a start, are exemplary; all meat and produce is sourced from strictly certified and approved suppliers, and The Deli itself is supervised under the London Beth Din. A large part of The Deli West One's success is down to the home-curing of its meats and particular salad and soup preparation. Salt beef, pastrami—both taken from the same brisket cut—turkey and tongue are brined on-site. The Deli's preparation of its salt beef and pastrami—inevitably two of the menus' most popular sandwiches—highlights their attention to detail. The former is steamed—not boiled, as is more common—straight from the brine. After brining, the pastrami is rubbed with The Deli's house season mix which includes black pepper, coriander, smoked paprika, garlic and other spices. Once this has had time to flavour, the briskets are then smoked slowly with wood chips before receiving a final steaming.

As well as these, other Jewish staples such as chopped liver, chicken soup with matza balls, latkes and pickles feature on the short but sweet menu.

Dinner
66 Knightsbridge
SW1X 7LA

020 7201 3833
www.dinnerbyheston.com

Dinner—Heston Blumenthal's first London venture—was named to represent the changing tastes and styles of historical British food. Contemporary nods to the past abound in both the décor and menu—dishes are dated with their approximate historical provenance and lighting is made from copies of elaborate jelly moulds. That is not to say that the food is simply a direct rehashing of Britain's past gastronomy. The much-written-about "Meat Fruit" exemplifies this: a shiny tangerine-like glazed sphere appears inconspicuous. But on breaking into the 'fruit', one discovers a chicken liver parfait, its sticky orange outer layer in fact a tart tangerine jelly that cuts though the creamy offal—an effective reworking of a fifteenth century favourite. Head Chef Ashley Palmer Watts and Blumenthal himself have tirelessly researched often forgotten dishes, cleverly reinventing them for modern palettes.

Huge windows provide views into both Hyde Park and the kitchen, where firewood is piled next to large wood-burning stoves, pineapples slowly roast on a spit and chefs work on preparing meticulous and lauded dishes. Despite the opulent setting, the set lunch menu is reasonably priced at £32 a head. The expensive à la carte, however, contains many idiosyncratic—and intriguingly named—plates, such as "Rice and flesh, c.1390"—and comprising saffron, calf tail and red wine—a "Black Foot pork chop, c.1860"—with spelt and Robert sauce, and a "Powdered duck breast, c.1670"—with smoked confit fennel and umbles.

DUKE OF CAMBRIDGE

Duke of Cambridge
30 St Peter's Street
N1 8JT

020 7359 3066
www.dukeorganic.co.uk

Restaurateur-environmentalist Geetie Singh opened Islington's Duke of Cambridge in 1998, with a remit dedicated to green practises, seasonal and welfare-conscious use of organic ingredients, and a focus on establishing a minimal carbon footprint by sourcing as much of its fresh produce and beer as locally as possible. Imported goods are kept to a minimum to reduce food miles, and wines are organic and biodynamically made. The pub has maintained its excellent credentials to this day, and is currently the only establishment of its kind in the UK to be certified by the Soil Association; appropriately, Singh was awarded an MBE in 2009 for services to the organic pub trade.

Luckily, the food as is as good as the Duke's ethics. Home-cured salt beef was a less yielding, more overtly English take on the traditional Jewish dish, suitably paired with a thick remoulade, capers and horseradish. Stewed venison, served with bubble and squeak and sweet red cabbage—an excellent foil to the earthy mushroom and juniper flavours in the sauce—was a tender and warming dish. A slab of pork belly had perfect crackling and looked a dream on the plate; it was complemented by vivid spring greens, roast potatoes and a rich tomato-based reduction. In a city blessed with numerous exponents of impressive British cooking, the Duke of Cambridge still stands out as one of the best.

THE EAGLE

The Eagle
159 Farringdon Road
EC1R 3AL

020 7837 1353

The Eagle—situated on a busy stretch of Farringdon Road, just south of Exmouth Market—opened in 1991, and is widely accepted as being London's first gastropub, an interesting accolade given the inescapable ubiquity of the trend now.

As you might expect, the dining room—that's all there is, excepting several cramped bar stools, a chesterfield sofa and a couple of picnic tables under the awning outside—is a bustling, clattery space, decorated in earthy tones, bare tables laden with mismatching cutlery and crockery, and menus scrawled on blackboards above the open kitchen.

Food is also rustic, indelicate and modern-European and British influenced. No surprises that The Eagle is owned by the team behind and affiliates of The Anchor & Hope, Great Queen Street and The Canton Arms. For a long time, The Eagle's most famous dish has been its "Bife Ana" steak sandwich: a small pile of thin beef rump marinated in garlic and oregano, topped with onions and slapped in a massive, lettuce-laced white roll. At £10 it's a little expensive, but well worth it. Despite the sandwich's dedicated following, the rest of The Eagle's offering should by no means be missed: braised, slow roasted and grilled meat and fish feature in some abundance, alongside comfort dishes such as "Neapolitan sausages with mashed potatoes, cabbage and creamed onions" and hearty Kedgeree, risottos and pasta dishes, amongst others on the frequently changing menu.

EYRE BROTHERS

Eyre Brothers
70 Leonard Street
EC2A 4QX

020 7613 5346
www.eyrebrothers.co.uk

David and Robert Eyre have some impressive culinary heritage in London—given that it was they who opened the Eagle in Clerkenwell—and Eyre Brothers, their quiet temple to Iberian cuisine, continues this in a respectable fashion. The menus reflect the brothers' upbringing in Mozambique, and David—as the establishment's Head Chef—has emphasised a focus on overwhelmingly domestic, authentically regional gastronomy at the restaurant. This is not to say that Eyre Brothers appears particularly rustic; the interior of the restaurant itself is resolutely slick, perhaps an inevitability given its position between the City and the yuppie enclave of Shoreditch.

Tapas and petiscos are available in the bar and lounge, but it's the meat dishes in the restaurant proper which have garnered the most acclaim, particularly Eyre's take on pork dishes; specifically, a dish of "Grilled fillet of acorn-fed Ibérico [Black Foot] pig", marinated with smoked paprika, thyme and garlic, and served with patatas pobres. Whilst Eyre Brothers is no longer the only purveyor of rare pork in the city—see Corner Room's much hyped, deconstructed example—it was one of the first, and it's become a classic signature dish of the restaurant. Ibérico pigs are suitable for cooking pink due to their free-roaming, semi-feral lives in rural Iberia; avoiding stys means a dearth of the bacteria which renders most pork unsuitable for cooking rare, whilst the free-range lifestyle of the pigs afford a marbling of fat through the meat unseen in other breeds.

FRANKLINS

Franklins
157 Lordship Lane
East Dulwich
SE22 8HX

020 8299 9598
www.franklinsrestaurant.com

Opened in 1999 by Rodney Franklin and Tim Sheehan, Franklins is an excellent example of an archetypal St John-indebted neighbourhood restaurant. We say indebted; critical acclaim would suggest that the cooking at Franklins could pip Henderson and co at their own game, their offal-heavy dishes more subtly embellished than the elegantly simply fare over in Clerkenwell.

The pretty dining room is quietly formal, pairing white-linen covered tables and clattering wooden chairs with art-bedecked bare-brick walls. The menu is British through and through. Vegetable produce is strictly seasonal, fish is ethically sourced from replenishable British stocks, and farms in the south of England supply the rare breed meat. Menus change daily and typical dishes might include rolled pig's spleen, salt beef hash, calf's faggots, ox tongue or rabbit with cider, carrots and baby turnips. Perennial side dishes include Scotch woodcock and thick slabs of gravy slathered black pudding on toast. The clear highlight of our visit was an exemplary dish of pan-fried calf's liver with pease pudding, sage and bacon, which was as aesthetically pleasing as it was punchily delicious. Prices are reasonable given the high standard of the cooking, with starters mostly costing £8 and mains hovering around the £16 mark.

As well as an intimate dinner location, the restaurant functions as a relaxed breakfast destination —one of the best in London according to *The Guardian* —and has a cosy, interestingly stocked bar.

THE HARWOOD ARMS

The Harwood Arms
27 Walham Grove
SW6 1QR

020 7386 1847
www.harwoodarms.com

The first gastropub in London to have been awarded a Michelin star, The Harwood Arms in Fulham is one of the finest exponents of British cooking in the capital. A joint venture between The Ledbury's Brett Graham, publican Edwin Vaux and Mike Graham of the highly regarded Pot Kiln in Berkshire, the pub-restaurant has maintained a near-faultless level of consistency and regard since opening in a renovated boozer in September 2008.

The pub sources exclusively British ingredients. Game is perhaps the biggest draw—as reflected in the photography decorating the smart, rustic dining room—though fish, seasonal vegetables and all other sundries are of an incredibly high standard. The dishes based around venison are the pub's most lauded; the adapted scotch egg served as a bar snack is truly outstanding. An exemplary main of "Grilled chop and crispy shoulder of Berkshire roe deer with field mushrooms and garlic potatoes" was a beautiful plate, the rare chop laden with wild mushrooms and set off with the croquette-like form of the shoulder meat. Perhaps even more impressive than the integrative sourcing of produce generally, Robinson shoots all the deer for the pub himself.

Other dishes including a bar snack of "Rabbit rissole on liquorice with Oxford sauce", small plates of brawn and rabbit faggots, and mains such as "Blade of aged English beef with baked beetroot and smoked bone marrow", as examples, only provide further indication and intent of the pub's thrilling take on British cuisine.

HAWKSMOOR

Hawksmoor Spitalfields
157 Commercial Street
E1 6BJ

020 7426 4850 (Restaurant)
020 7426 4856 (Bar)
www.thehawksmoor.com

Hawksmoor Guildhall
10 Basinghall Street
EC2V 5BQ

020 7397 8120

Hawksmoor Seven Dials
11 Langley Street
WC2H 9JG

020 7420 9390

Few restaurants in the UK have gained such overwhelming acclaim as the small Hawksmoor group. Childhood friends Will Beckett and Huw Gott opened the inaugural branch near Spitalfields in June 2006; unlike now, still an area with a relative dearth of decent restaurants, save St John Bread & Wine and a few market stalwarts. The pair served "dictionary thick" 35-day (at least) dry aged steaks cooked over a charcoal grill; Tim Wilson's Ginger Pig supplied the meat from the outset.

The restaurant has been widely praised since its launch, with Giles Coren declaring it "Flawless. The best steak you'll find anywhere". Branches in Seven Dials and in the City at Guildhall—as well as a new, more casual basement bar at the first site—have since opened. All maintain the high standards of the Spitalfields restaurant.

All of the fare served at Hawksmoor has been hugely well received. Breakfasts—including the cheekily referential "Sausage and egg HK muffin" and the Hawksmoor breakfast for two, which includes "Short-rib bubble and squeak", bone marrow, black pudding and mutton, beef and pork sausages—are gaining infamy around the capital; the Sunday roast is considered one of the best in London; starters, mains and sides include such treats as "Bone marrow with onions", an acclaimed burger, and "Meatballs & Grits". And, of course, the steaks: from chateaubriand and porterhouse sold by the 100g, to bone-in sirloin and 55-day aged D-rump; all, to quote *Bloomberg*, "murderously good".

HEREFORD ROAD

Hereford Road
3 Hereford Road
Westbourne Grove
W2 4AB

020 7727 1144
www.herefordroad.org

Hereford Road is one of the more successful neighbourhood restaurants in London. Tom Pemberton, previously Head Chef at St John Bread & Wine in Spitalfields, maintains an excellent culinary output clearly indebted to his old boss Fergus Henderson. A dedication to seasonality, functionality and a ubiquitous use of offal may not be a rare sight these days, but Pemberton's cooking is some of the most satisfying in the city. Critical appraisals have been overwhelmingly positive, and the American chef Thomas Keller—he of the renowned French Laundry in California—named Hereford Road one of his favourite restaurants in a *Guardian* article a few years back.

As for the food: we tasted a dish of incredibly light and creamy "Calf's brains, fried in brown butter with capers" that was rich enough to stop one in their tracks, if it weren't for a perfectly cooked onglet steak to follow. The menu has included such simple, British plates as starters of "Lamb's sweetbreads, breast, green beans and mint" and "Duck livers with green beans and tarragon"; and mains such as "Barnsley chop, chard and anchovy" and "Guinea fowl, lentils and peas".

Given the quality of the cooking, prices at Hereford Road are impressively reasonable. Starters and deserts—excepting a decent cheese selection—top out at £7.50, and mains for one are around £14.

HIX OYSTER & CHOP HOUSE

Hix Oyster & Chop House
36–37 Greenhill Rents
Cowcross Street
EC1M 6BN

020 7017 1930
www.hixoysterandchophouse.co.uk

HIX
66–70 Brewer Street
W1F 9UP

020 7292 3518
www.hixsoho.co.uk

Tramshed
32 Rivington Street
EC2A 3LX

020 7749 0478
www.chickenandsteak.co.uk

One of London's best-known chefs, man-about-town Mark Hix garnered 17 years under his belt as Executive Head Chef of Caprice Holdings—meaning he has fed just about every mover and shaker to pass through London since 1990—before opening his first restaurant, Hix Oyster & Chop House, in 2008. He has since grown a stable of restaurants to rival his old employer, and he recently opened a new venture, Tramshed, in Shoreditch.

For the meat-loving gastronome, however, first stop should be Hix's inaugural establishment, the aforementioned Oyster & Chop House, situated metres from the historic Smithfield meat market. Beef features heavily on the menu, alongside variations on traditional British foul, chops, pies and sausages, incorporating provenance-specific dishes such as "Moyallon sweet-cure bacon chop with Herefordshire snails and alexanders" and "Goosnargh chicken salad with Sillfield Farm bacon and sweetcorn fritters". Steak enthusiasts can choose between porterhouse, fillet or rib steak on the bone, though the lauded signature dish of Hanger steak—otherwise known as skirt or onglet, as seen in so many French bistros—with baked bone marrow is highly deserving of the praise received (and is one of the cheaper dishes on the menu). If this all seems a little flesh-heavy, the starters menu offers more in the way of vegetable and seafood options, although the rock oysters, still served with spicy sausage and "Brookfield Farm veal dumpling with creamed savoy cabbage" are a tempting option.

HONEST BURGERS

Honest Burgers
Unit 12
Brixton Village
SW9 8PR

020 7733 7963
www.honestburgers.co.uk

The cafe-centric redevelopment of and ensuing blogger-frenzy over Brixton Village has been pretty miraculous in regenerating the southern end of gritty Coldharbour Lane. Well, for roaming gastronomes at least. The amazing sourdough pizza over at Franco Manca made it the first critical darling of the area—who ever expected a cramped unit in Brixton Market to appear in *Bloomberg*?— but the Village's myriad eateries are quickly gaining a name for themselves. Mid-market burger start-ups are nothing new in London these days—blame Yanni Papoutsis and his original Meat Wagon if you like— but Honest Burgers is pretty near the apex of a very crowded scene. They don't take bookings—seemingly largely inescapable—though they will take your number and let you run to the nearest pub. Crucially, the food is well worth the inevitable wait.

The menu is short and to the point: three beef burgers, a changing special, a chicken sandwich and a vegetarian fritter. The eponymous "Honest" burger, topped with smoked bacon, mature cheddar and pickled cucumbers is in serious danger of being the best in London. House chips—here included in the price and elsewhere often an afterthought— are equally as moreish, pre-salted and covered in rosemary. Honest Burgers' claims of inspiration derived from "Great British Produce" is substantiated in its sourcing of all their meat from the ever-reliable Ginger Pig. In addition, and luckily for the wheat-intolerant amongst us, they also have the option of gluten free buns as an alternative to the regular brioche number.

The Ledbury
127 Ledbury Road
W11 2AQ

020 7792 9090
www.theledbury.com

The Ledbury—in Notting Hill—opened in 2005. The Australian Brett Graham has been Head Chef since its inception, following his first UK stint under Philip Howard at The Square, during which time he was awarded Young Chef of the Year in 2002. His work at The Ledbury has seen the restaurant ranked fourteenth in the world by San Pellegrino's global rankings; by *The Times* as the finest in the country; and as the best in London by *Hardens* and *Zagat*. It has earned exclusively excellent critical praise and been awarded two Michelin stars. No small feat.

Graham's menus at The Ledbury are modern, French-inspired and subtly complex, with food given an Antipodean twist. Mains are largely meat-focussed and explicitly reflect his personal interest in hunting, with an abundance of game and seasonal plates. Saddle of Berkshire roe buck is elegantly paired with sweet white beetroot, red wine lees and a hit of smoked bone marrow; delicate rump of veal is both poached and roasted, matched with wild garlic, creamed potato and heady spring truffle; pigeon also features heavily, when we tried it with foie gras and cherry blossom. Intriguingly, loin and shoulder of biodynamic hogget is also offered, with an aubergine glazed in black sugar and garlic. Prices aren't low —the à la carte menu is £80 for three courses, the tasting menu £105 for nine (without drinks). For some there is, fortunately, an excellent, much written-about set lunch menu of three-courses for £35.

Magdalen
152 Tooley Street
SE1 2TU

020 7403 1342
www.magdalenrestaurant.co.uk

Since opening in 2007, the Magdalen, near London Bridge, has been garnering ever-increasing acclaim for its dedication to honest, wholesome cooking. Three of the restaurant's four founders—specifically James and Emma Faulks and David Abbott, the fourth being James' father Roger—met at La Trompette in Chiswick (itself a de facto offshoot of Wandsworth's perennially popular Chez Bruce and Kew's The Glasshouse), and their collective heritage includes stints at The Fat Duck, The Anchor & Hope, the Mandarin Oriental and Le Manoir Aux Quat' Saisons.

Much has been written of this pedigree and of the Magdalen's merging of traditional modern European and British tropes in its cooking. Though the restaurant's "Venison and trotter pie" is now the stuff of critical legend, the rest of its seasonally changing menus evince this more explicitly. Starters include such dishes such as "Fried calves brains, capers and sage" —a dish reminiscent of the cooking of other local protégés of Fergus Henderson, further supported by James' aforementioned time under Jonathon Jones at The Anchor & Hope—and "Rabbit and trotter ragu, white polenta and parmesan". Mains might encompass "Grilled veal heart, duck fat potato cake and béarnaise", an oxtail and kidney pudding or "Slow cooked suckling kid neck, white beans, fennel and wild garlic". The Magdalen hits the middle ground of affordability with three courses à la carte costing around £35, though the three course set-lunch for £18.50 is excellent value.

MANGAL 2

Mangal 2
4 Stoke Newington Road
N16 8BH

020 7254 7888
www.mangal2.com

Despite its innocuous appearance and busy, relatively grimy location in Dalston, Mangal 2 Ocakbasi is one of the most highly regarded Turkish/Kurdish restaurants in London. The Ocakbasi of the name translates literally to "at the grill"; traditionally, people would sit around such grills and observe their meat, vegetables and salad being prepared. Ali Dirik's initial modern appropriation—the Mangal Restaurant on nearby Arcola Street, opened in 1990—was the first of its kind in the UK. Dirik no longer manages that site, but opened Mangal 2 nearby in 1994.

Meze, stews and salads are all represented in the extensive menu, but it's the grilled meats that are the real draw. Lamb chops, lamb ribs, sweetbreads (Uykuluk), liver (Cigar Sis), kidneys (Bobrek), quail (Bildercin), chicken, Turkish beef sausages and various fish are grilled with natural wood charcoal over an open fire; a far cry from your standard ubiquitous London kebab shop. For cultural kudos, it's also well known that Gilbert & George eat there most evenings.

Meatballs
92–94 Farringdon Road
EC1R 3EA

020 3490 6228
www.meatballs.co.uk

Meatballs—located in the listed Victorian surroundings of what was the Quality Chop House, just round the corner from Exmouth Market on Farringdon Road—has, perhaps unsurprisingly given the name, quite the limited remit in its fare. Not that this is a bad thing when the food is this satisfying. The menu (also available for a decent lunchtime takeaway) consists of five constant balls—"Beef and ricotta", "Greek lamb", "Thai chilli chicken", "Pork and rosemary" and "Vegetarian courgette balls"—and a weekly "guest" meatball made, excepting the vegetarian number, from free range pork, Orkney beef and lamb and Banhams poultry, all supplied by local butchers, Barratts of Englands Lane.

The balls are served either as is; as a burger; with an "Underneath"—mash, a pearl barley risotto, spaghetti or, most enticingly, egg pappardelle with a parmesan cream; or as last year's most popular fad, "Sliders"—single meatballs in petit home made bread buns.

Starters and sides—from Caesar salad and "Chop House prawn cocktail" through fries and peas with lettuce, spring onions and cream—are reliably perfunctory, though deserts such as a "Chocolate brownie ice cream sandwich" and "Aunt Joyce's baked egg custard" afford a more retro nod to the restaurant's American air.

MEAT LIQUOR

Meat Liquor
74 Welbeck Street
W1G 0BA

No phone
www.meatliquor.com

If you haven't yet eaten at one of Yianni Papoutsis' burger ventures, you can't reasonably call yourself a foodie Londoner. His original set-up, the Meat Wagon, can be credited with kickstarting the current transcendence of hamburgers from generic fast food staple to gourmet menu item du jour. Meateasy, the pop up restaurant he ran above an abandoned pub, managed to lure every food critic in town to the insalubrious surrounds of New Cross. So it's really no surprise that the opening of a permanent restaurant in Marylebone devoted to his burgers caused quite a stir. With a characteristic directness and simplicity, Meat Liquor provides exactly what its name suggests: excellent burgers, accompanied by delicious cocktails, made with ice chipped straight from the block and served in jam jars. Starters and sides are a mixed bag; deep-fried pickles are hot, crunchy, tangy and unexpectedly delicious while the fries—excepting those covered in chilli—are a little so-so. However, it's the burgers that have garnered endless acclaim and deservedly so. Predominantly built around the classic cheeseburger with various combinations encompassing pickles, bacon, chilli and sauces to complement, the pure chuck steak patties are succulent, juicy and pleasingly sloppy; you will use most of the kitchen roll provided in place of napkins. Be warned though, Meat Liquor's no reservations policy—and its ensuing status as one of the hippest eateries in town—ensures hefty queues and long waits for dinner.

MISHKIN'S

Mishkin's
25 Catherine Street
WC2B 5JS

020 7240 2078
www.mishkins.co.uk

Calling itself a "kind of Jewish deli", Mishkin's is currently Russell Norman's newest restaurant venture—he of Polpo, Polpetto, Spuntino and Da Polpo fame, and "currently" because his small group-cum-chain seems to constantly have a new opening simmering away—and takes its cues from the traditional New York delis of legend and gives them a welcome twist. Named after the apocryphal E Mishkin—fictitious founder of the establishment —the diner-like restaurant deals in the sort of food normally served in gargantuan portions: not necessarily a move one might have expected from a group that is more widely known for its hand in starting the conspicuous 'small plates' revolution in London. However, treated with Norman and his team's customary skill and attention to detail, this new direction is a quiet, if admittedly non-Kosher, success. Sandwiches—inevitably the most tempting items on the menu—are largely traditionally influenced, from a Brick Lane salt beef and mustard number and an excellent "Reuben on rye with pastrami, sauerkraut, Russian dressing and Swiss cheese" to chopped chicken liver with "schmaltzed radish" and a small but intense steamed patty burger with onions and Swiss cheese. There is also chicken matzo ball soup and latkes with smoked trout to satisfy any Lower East Side cravings. Their all-day brunch and supper lists are satisfyingly heavy and comforting —including meat loaf and corn dogs. There is also a meatball list and numerous daily specials.

OPERA TAVERN

Opera Tavern
23 Catherine Street
WC2B 5JS

020 7836 3680
www.operatavern.co.uk

As part of the well-regarded Salt Yard Group, Covent Garden's Opera Tavern has esteemed company in the small plate Iberia-cum-Italian stalwarts Salt Yard and Dehesa.

Focussing on charcuterie, cheeses and well-considered tapas-sized dishes, Simon Mullins' and Sanja Morris' restaurant has been praised for its dedication to smart but unpretentious food, cosily grown-up aesthetic and thoughtful sourcing of ingredients; a world away from most of the generic, drab eateries in and around Covent Garden.

The grilled "Mini Ibérico pork and foie gras burger" with melted manchego and caramelised red onion, and cured hams are ostensibly the Opera Tavern's best known items but the menu is a relative riot of gutsy grills, bar snacks and tapas plates: "House recipe brawn", from Catalunya; skewers of "Calves' liver with trevise and aged balsamic" and "Moorish marinated Ibérico pork"; glorified pork scratchings in "Crispy Ibérico pigs ears"; and "Confit of Old Spot pork belly with rosemary scented cannellini beans" all feature alongside lighter—inevitably less meaty—fare such as the Salt Yard classic of "Courgette flowers stuffed with goats' cheese and drizzled with honey" and Italian and Spanish cheeses.

Excluding a comparatively small number of spirits, fortified wines and regular bottles, the extensive wine and sherry list is overwhelmingly Spanish and Italian, an impressive and tempting draw to the Opera Tavern in itself.

PITT CUE CO.

Pitt Cue Co.
1 Newburgh Street
W1F 7RB

020 7287 5578
www.pittcue.co.uk

After spending a summer dishing up acclaimed barbecue fare from a converted burger van under the South Bank side of Hungerford Bridge, Tom Adams and Jamie Berger set up a permanent incarnation of Pitt Cue Co. in a tiny shop between Soho and Carnaby Street. The pair could largely claim to be spearheading the zeitgeist for considered, US-indebted barbecue food, now an increasingly common sight in the capital with the conspicuous arrival of De Beauvoir's Duke's Brew & Que, Jamie Oliver's Barbecoa, Red Dog Saloon in Shoreditch and the established Bodean's chain.

A tiny upstairs bar area belies a sparsely decorated basement restaurant almost as miniature, boasting seating for a mere 24 people. The informality of the space complements the food though; refined and delicate Pitt Cue Co. is not. Meals are served in prison-style enamel trays and portions are gargantuan. The ribs are huge, yielding hunks of hot-smoked and hickory roasted beef, stickily glazed and perfectly charred. Pulled pork, sausages, smoked hot chicken wings, ox cheek and beef brisket also feature on the changing menu, and are complemented by zingy slaws, pickles, wedges of grilled sourdough and generous sides such as "Burnt end mash"—creamy mashed potato topped with caramelised brisket ends.

There's a no bookings policy, obviously, but the bar-cum-queuing area is interestingly stocked, with local Kernel beers and shooters such as the infamous "Pickleback"; a shot of bourbon coupled with one of warm pickle brine.

POPESEYE

Popeseye
108 Blythe Road
Kensington Olympia
W14 0HD

020 7610 4578
www.popeseye.com

277 Upper Richmond Road
SW15 6SP

020 8788 7733

Named after a Scottish term for a thinly steak cut from the middle of the cow's rump, Popeseye—in both its Putney and Olympia incarnations—is a critically acclaimed, if under-reported institution, preceding Hawksmoor, Buen Ayre et al for an attempt on the best steak in London. "Purist" might be an understated term to apply to the restaurants' remit; the menu is so succinct as to appear almost flippant, with three cuts (sirloin, the titular popeseye/rump and fillet) each in five weights—from a dainty six ounces through to a daunting 30—and served with chips, a simply dressed salad, a hefty range of mustards, béarnaise sauce and ketchup. All of the meat sold is purely grass-fed Aberdeen Angus, and hung for at least 28 days. Puddings are resolutely home made and in huge portions, cheeses perfectly kept, and the wine list happily errs towards appropriate Clarets and Burgundys, though it does venture as far afield as Lebanon, in addition to a good selection of New World bottles. The dining room itself is functional in a charming retro-bistro fashion, recently adorned with a nice selection of bovine-centric art.

The high quality of the beef—and keen skill of chef-owner Ian Huchinson—has earned Popeseye some lofty accolades; that Jay Rayner once labelled it "the Holy Grail" of steak houses is no faint praise.

THE RIDING HOUSE CAFE

The Riding House Cafe
43–51 Great Titchfield Street
W1W 7PQ

020 7927 0840
www.ridinghousecafe.co.uk

A self-styled "modern all-day brasserie", Great Titchfield Street's Riding House Cafe provides satisfying fare for roving gastronomes, hungry shoppers and the local office workers of Fitzrovia. Breakfasts include a traditional full English, an "Orkney Bacon Sandwich" served on white bread with the welcome addition of avocado, and "Eggs Hussard"—with ox heart tomato, ham, spinach, bordelaise and hollandaise. Lighter cereals and smoothies also feature. Lunch and dinner menus offer an excellent burger and a strong line in steak—with a chateaubriand to share, or choices of rib eye on the bone and Aberdeen Angus sirloin, both served with béarnaise sauce—and comfort food such as "Grilled lamb chump chops" and "Pan fried liver and bacon", with sweet and sour peppers, onions and polenta. A "Chorizo hash brown" with mushrooms and a poached egg are also available as a hangover cure at the start of the day and again as a comforting meal at lunch and dinner. Also prevalent are small plates, priced at £4–6 amongst which the current trend for Southern cooking is given a nod with a dish of "Spicy buttermilk fried chicken with celery and blue cheese". A walk-in bar area alongside the booking restaurant make this a handy spot to drop by when in central London.

Also alluring, and a complement to the food, is the Cafe's décor: a striking mix of panelled gentleman's club-cum-diner and a more slick, industrial-tinged eatery.

ROAST

Roast
The Floral Hall
Stoney Street
SE1 1TL

0845 0347300
www.roast-restaurant.co.uk

An established stop on the gastro-tourist's London list, Roast—impressively situated in Borough Market's converted Floral Hall, a location which affords views over the market itself and further afield—nevertheless justifies its lasting popularity and somewhat above-average prices. Opened in 2006 by Iqbal Wahhab OBE, the restaurant cites an ongoing dedication to traditional, specifically British cooking, making use of local and seasonal ingredients in its elegant, yet gutsy, menus; provenance is conspicuous in the descriptions of the dishes, and many of the ingredients are purportedly sourced from the market stalls surrounding it.

Inevitably, meat is the key focus here; starters could include adapted classics such as "Irish salt beef croquettes with whipped peas and dandelion", and "Scotch Burford Brown egg with Macsween haggis and caper mayonnaise".

Mains are less delicate still: "Herb-roasted fillet of Whitestone Cliff Longhorn with beef dripping roasted potatoes and Yorkshire pudding", "Chargrilled Launceston lamb neck fillet with a spelt, lemon and herb salad and cucumber yoghurt" and a hefty "Yorkshire Longhorn T-bone steak with scrumpy-battered onion rings" sit alongside a goat curry and a chicken, snail and leek pie. In addition, the Sunday roast is considered one of the best in London. Vegetarian dishes, although numerous, have been considered a possible afterthought to the main meaty deal here in some critical circles. Given the restaurant's nomenclature, one must wonder why anyone would have imagined otherwise.

ROCHELLE CANTEEN

Rochelle Canteen
Rochelle School
Arnold Circus
E2 7ES

020 7729 5677
www.arnoldandhenderson.com

Melanie Arnold and Margot Henderson's Rochelle Canteen—situated in a renovated bicycle shed in the grounds of the Rochelle School in Shoreditch—is something of a hidden treasure for the knowing food enthusiast. The dining room—open weekday breakfasts and lunchtimes only, and accessible by ringing a bell for entry—is plain and unfussy, an understated space of simple tables and wooden chairs alongside an open kitchen, and largely patronised by the local artistic community. The Canteen's menus stylistically follow suit, and—in the St John tradition of stoic, steadfast functionality—list simply the basic ingredients of the seasonally focussed, 'nose-to-tail'-centric food. Thus, "Terrine" or "Rillette and pickled chicory" could be followed by "Devilled kidney on toast", "Grilled lamb leg, new potato and green sauce" or "Tamworth, pearl barley and runner beans". That Margot Henderson is the wife of St John's Fergus may perhaps be unsurprising to some, but the Canteen is a lauded, highly successful establishment even without the worthy familial associations.

RULES

Rules
35 Maiden Lane
WC2E 7LB

020 7836 5314
www.rules.co.uk

Rules is the kind of restaurant in which it would be perfectly possible to imagine oneself transported back to the middle of the last century, drinking French wine poured by a gloved waiter, eating game served in polished containers or steak and kidney pudding with proper silverware, immersed in a general air of old fashioned Britishness (and surrounded by antlers). To some, this is its best feature; to others, its most grating. But wherever you stand on old-world traditions, décor and etiquette, Rules is rightly known for its food, and in particular, its meat.

Established in 1798 by Thomas Rule—making it the oldest restaurant in London— Rules boasts its own estate in the Pennines, Lartington. Game is therefore a must, and the seasonally driven menus regularly feature the likes of partridge, woodcock, ptarmigan, pheasant and red deer. The downstairs kitchen also houses a butchery, long before they became trendy must-haves for certain celebrity chefs. Animals are bought in whole, from which all cuts and offal are used. The recent transformation of the upstairs bar, replete with classic and good value bar menu is the antidote to busy Covent Garden: a country house bar in the heart of London that does a fine Negroni.

Unlike many London restaurants, where tradition appears to have been delivered en masse and applied liberally to the walls by the latest hip design team, Rules is the genuine article. To eat here is to join the long list of patrons, which includes nine monarchs, Charles Dickens, Lawrence Olivier, Buster Keaton and Kingsley Amis.

SIMPSON'S-IN-THE-STRAND

Simpson's-in-the-Strand
100 Strand
WC2R 0EW

020 7836 9112
www.simpsonsinthestrand.co.uk

Simpson's-in-the-Strand is a long-established London institution, where gentlemen and tourists have breakfasted and had their Sunday roasts carved at the table for the last 170 years. It was originally a chess club and coffee house that served food, and it is here that the concept of the carvery began—as a way to serve customers without disturbing their games.

Simpson's provides archetypally British food, sourced locally. The menu features plates such as calf's liver steak, stuffed suckling pig and aged Scottish steaks, but it is most famous and most often frequented for its famous carvery dishes. With these, a huge cut of roast beef is wheeled to your table under a vast silver dome and artfully sliced onto your plate with classic British—as in, notably understated—theatricality. Service is courteous and your gravy—not jus—will be brought thick and in a jug. Tradition oozes from the menu, from its use of the title "Master Cook" to its almost reductively retro side dishes.

Simpson's-in-the-Strand isn't cheap, but most are aware that you're paying for character and style as much as food. Portions, however, are generous. For anyone particularly enthusiastic about roast meats, gift vouchers are available for carving courses, where customers are taught to carve four different cuts, served lunch afterwards and presented with their own carving set and certificate.

SPUNTINO

Spuntino
61 Rupert Street
Soho W1D 7PW

No phone
www.spuntino.co.uk

Small plates? Check. No reservations? Check. Burgers? Well, of a sort. Spuntino ticks all the boxes for fashionable destinations in London at the moment but, as sister-restaurant to Soho favourites Polpo and Polpetto, it does so with aplomb. It is the slightly grungier sibling, playing it cool with a minimalist website, no phone number or email address—you have to be in the know to eat here—distressed décor and an American slant to the 'hangover food' menu that is where those almost-burgers come in. Spuntino has become renowned for its "Sliders", the couple-of-bites-sized burgers made here with salt beef (from the Brick Lane bagel bakery), lamb and pickled cucumber or pulled pork with pickled apple. The joy of this diminutive sizing is that you can order one of each without breaking body or bank. They are complemented by a selection of dishes providing a similar twist on diner food: truffled egg toast, steak and eggs, buttermilk chicken and stuffed fried olives all provide flavoursome nuggets of food that can act as perfect bar snacks—ideal as most punters will find themselves perched at this, as there is only one table proper—or as a more substantial meal. With just the right amount of grease and salt, Spuntino is indeed an excellent location, either to soak up today's hangover or start work on tomorrow's.

St John Bar & Restaurant
26 St John Street
EC1M 4AY

020 3301 8069
www.stjohnrestaurant.com

St John Bread & Wine
94 Commercial Street
E1 6LZ

020 3301 8020
www.stjohnbreadandwine.com

St John Hotel
1 Leicester Street
WC2H 7BL

020 3301 8069
www.stjohnhotellondon.com

Fergus Henderson and Trevor Gulliver opened the original Clerkenwell branch of St John in 1994. Since then, they have expanded to included St John Bread & Wine in Spitalfields, the St John Hotel in Soho and the St John Bakery at Maltby Street in Bermondsey, though the initial site is still the integral cog in their miniature—but highly influential—empire. Where many of its contemporaries enjoy a vocal, self-serving relationship with 'new' trends in unconventional meat-eating in the media, St John's strong point is its consistent, subtle dedication to quietly plugging away doing exactly what it has been for the last two decades. The menu changes constantly according to seasonality, and Henderson's support for 'nose-to-tail' eating, paired with the inclination to in-house butchery at the restaurant, means that dishes are decided on the spur of the moment and often of rarely used cuts of the animal. Certainly, there are few establishments in London serving parts such as bone marrow—here a signature dish—tripe and ox heart as often and as brilliantly. The somewhat rickety, canteen-style interior of the restaurant also sees dishes such as "Pigeon and beetroot", "Crispy pig skin and dandelion", "Braised hare and swede" and "Veal chop, chicory and anchovy" served on a daily basis. The menu reads as a stoically basic list of ingredients, highlighting the team's outstanding skills in making the most of a simple number of ingredients cooked exceptionally well. It's no surprise that St John has consistently made the upper echelons of critics' world restaurant lists since opening.

TRULLO

Trullo
300 Saint Paul's Road
N1 2LH

020 7226 2733
www.trullorestaurant.com

Opened in June 2010 by Tim Siadatan, one of Jamie Oliver's original Fifteen, Trullo introduced some deservedly hyped fine dining to the 'other end' of Upper Street, providing a welcome respite to the polluted chaos of Highbury Corner. Following his stint with Oliver, Siadatan then worked at both Moro and St John, so the restaurant's focus on fresh, simple flavours comes as no surprise. The Italian-inspired menu, featuring antipasti, hand-made pasta, and meat and fish cooked over their charcoal grill changes daily, meaning that the food on your plate will be the best of the season.

As one would expect with authentic Italian fare, Trullo's menus lend themselves to long, drawn-out, multiple course meals. An "Antipasti of chargrilled ox heart with marinated red peppers" or "Grilled quail with chicken liver crostini" might come before a pasta course of "Pappardelle with beef shin ragu". Mains are either cooked in the oven, like the "Braised Swaledale lamb shoulder with Jersey Royals and braised spring peas", or else over the grill as with "Beef onglet with chickpea, fried aubergine and oregano dressing". A quieter downstairs restaurant offers a similar, if abbreviated, menu, focusing on small plates, alongside cocktails which take their cues from the Italian flavours and ingredients featured in the food. Perhaps the best way to enjoy the rustic Italian fare on offer is to linger with a group of friends or family over the set four-course Sunday lunch.

Ox cheek, mushrooms and polenta from Tongue 'n Cheek, Eat St

STREET FOOD

BIG APPLE HOT DOGS

Big Apple Hot Dogs
239 Old Street
EC1V 9EY

Eat St
Kings Boulevard
N1C
www.eat.st

07989 387441
www.bigapplehotdogs.com

Big Apple Hot Dogs has made quite a name for itself in London, its steadfast Old Street-based hub attracting a steady stream of lunching types and in-the-know street food enthusiasts. Owner Abiye Cole has devised four worthy and specially commissioned varieties—"The Big Dog", "The Pimp Steak", "The Big Frank" and "Frank Junior", which are lovingly nestled in a softer than soft white bun and accompanied by a choice of condiments.

"The Big Dog" is an all-beef giant, seasoned with garlic, paprika and black pepper, giving it more texture than your average hotdog. "The Pimp Steak" is "pimped" with the addition of oak smoked pork and paprika, nutmeg and pepper. Softer than its beef brother, it's the perfect halfway house for those not wanting to veer too far from the familiar porky frankfurter. For real fanatics however, "The Big Frank" is not just a must-have: it's a bona fide experience. For starters, it's massive. It's also one of the juiciest frankfurters out there, and, being made of 100 per cent oak-smoked pork seasoned with spices, it's one of the tastiest. If for some unforeseen reason you think it's too large you can opt for the children's version, "Frank Jnr"—same taste, only smaller. With classic condiments—German and American variations included—and generous helpings of sweet fried onions provided, you'll be satisfied whether you prefer your sausages to hail from Frankfurt or Brooklyn.

THE BOWLER

The Bowler
Eat St
Kings Boulevard
N I C
www.eat.st

07815 154995
www.thebowleruk.tumblr.com

A dedicated gourmet meatball outfit—though owner Jez Felwick has been known to say "if it can be made round, it's in"—The Bowler produces a delicious array of meaty spheres, as well as vegetarian alternatives. Double entendres abound in the glowing press for this distinctive ex-ice cream van covered in astroturf—the "Lawn Ranger"—where you can feast on tasty fare made from proper cuts of meat, deftly rolled into balls and cooked before your eyes.

Felwick makes street food meatballs for a number of reasons. For starters they're crowd pleasers, the stuff of happy memories—big bowls of meatballs slathered in sauce—but he's keen to give this happy association a gourmet twist. By using top-quality meats and taking international flavour inspiration, the potential variations are endless. One of the delights of street food is the enthusiastic proprietor's quest for the wittiest dish titles, and Felwick is no exception: "Great Balls of Fire" is an instant classic made from minced pork shoulder and beef chuck served with a spiced onion and tomato sauce; "Bjorn Balls" is a Scandinavian take on the meatball, served with mash, a zingy cucumber pickle and lingonberry jam; and the much tweeted about "ExciThaiBall" is a sweet, spicy and sticky green chilli and ginger pork ball in coconut curry sauce. Obligatory innuendos aside, The Bowler's balls are a sight to behold. Watch out for the new bacon concoction, comprising beef chuck, paprika and pancetta.

BRINDISA CHORIZO GRILL

Brindisa Chorizo Grill
18–20 Southwark Street
(Next to Tapas Brindisa)

020 7357 8880
www.brindisa.com

The concept behind Brindisa's Chorizo Grill is simple: the finest ingredients, cooked simply in front of the customer and at reasonable prices. They do one thing—their much-lauded Chorizo sandwich—and do it so well that it has been called "pure perfection" and "a five-star snack" by the press. Unsurprisingly, suspiciously similar sandwiches are becoming ubiquitous around the capital. No bad thing really.

The grill is a simple four-foot by six-foot space located next to Brindisa's deli at bustling Borough Market, which in busy times is occupied by four staff. No matter how packed the market is, a wait is always inevitable.

Their secret: they use Alejandro Barbacoa chorizo from a supplier who has been working with Brindisa since it began. Made with a Riojan recipe, passed down through four generations of the Rituerto family, from hand-trimmed cuts of pork seasoned with smoked paprika—the distinguished Pimenton de la Vera—it is free from additives and preservatives. Stuffed in the classic ciabatta roll along with the hot griddled chorizo are sweet piquillo peppers from Brindisa's supplier Navarrico. It is then generously covered with peppery rocket and drizzled with Arbequin and Picual olive oil. Although they don't vary their offerings, it is possible to double the chorizo, which, far from putting the sandwich out of balance, really reveals that there are times when double chorizo is a must —particularly on Saturdays for an early lunch.

BRINDISA
SPANISH FOODS

DADDY DONKEY

Daddy Donkey
Pitches 100–101 Leather Lane
EC1N 7TE

020 7267 6042
www.daddydonkey.co.uk

'Burrito' in Spanish literally means 'little donkey'. Daddy Donkey, therefore, intends to make the father of all burritos, and the stall has rightly come a long way from its humble beginnings. The owner, Joel Henderson, set up on Leather Lane when he finished university with "just a rickety wooden market barrow, a couple of Argos camping stoves, a stripy blue and white tarpaulin and one member of staff". He muses that it "seems ludicrous when I think about it now, but somehow we made it work".

Having loved the culture of street food in Mexico while studying abroad, Henderson decided to bring some of it London's way by using authentic, natural and fresh Mexican flavours. For Henderson, Mexican food is all about the salsa, which, he says, "adds freshness, zest, spiciness and gets all over the place!" This asides, Daddy Donkey's two takes on beef are particularly worth a mention. The "Tamatillo" is a shredded beef brisket number cooked in tamatillo chile de arbol and coriander salsa; the slightly softer "Picadillo" is made from ground beef slow-cooked in Daddy Donkey's special blend of spices and chipotle salsa.

Henderson's signature, though, is the Daddy D burrito. As the name suggests, it's huge and filled with rice and black beans, a choice of meat, hot salsa made from their combination of habanero and toasted chile de arbol chillies, cheese, lettuce and their famous "holy guacamole".

DOGFATHER DINER

Dogfather Diner
North Cross Road Market East
Dulwich
SE22

07939 474320
www.dogfatherdiner.com

When Cooper Deville decided to start his own street food stall, he realised that to do well he needed to take one concept, keep it simple and really make it his own. Realising that the American favourite, the hotdog, had been either over-looked or done so badly that it was no longer worth considering a proper hotdog, he set about rectifying the situation by starting Dogfather Diner—the quirkiest, tastiest hotdog stall in town.

Deville uses Kosher beef dogs, supplied by his enigmatic "Jewish Hotdog Man", because the flavour really stands out against the often dubiously-made high pork and fat alternatives. The dog is free from any kind of mechanically reclaimed meat or over-processed content and consequently has a great flavour. With a constantly changing selection of specials, ranging from the "Mexican Elvis"—made with homemade chilli, melting cheese, jalapenos and hot sauce—to the "Snoop Dog" with streaky bacon, barbecue sauce and creamed corn mayo, there is something for everyone. The ever-popular "Dogfather" has become Deville's signature dog— the first "haute dog" to go on the menu and still a winner, it is stuffed in a made-to-order bun, coated with sweet and spicy chorizo slices and melted mozzarella. It is then slathered with soft grilled onions, fiery jalapenos and a homemade roasted red pepper marinara, all topped off with a sprinkling of salty parmesan.

Kimchi Cult
Chatsworth Road Market
Chatsworth Road
E5
www.chatsworthroade5.co.uk

Eat St
Kings Boulevard
N1C
www.eat.st

No phone
www.kimchicult.com

Kimchi Cult's food is a cultural mix-up between Korean and Mexican classics, with the a focus on the stall's tangy and hot homemade kimchi—a traditional Korean condiment made of fermented vegetables—the flavours of which are taken as the base point for dishes like "Kimchi Sliders", and pulled pork with kimchi, guacamole, cheese and jalapenos. The bulgogi steak sub is another favourite—juicy, sweet and soaked with at tangy pear, soy and sesame marinade. Combining the trans-Pacific flavours of Mexico and Korea, all dishes are a satisfying and delicious balance of the hot, sweet, sour and salty.

Kimchi Cult was started by Danny O'Sullivan, who was inspired by the buzz of the street food stalls in Korea, which he discovered while teaching English, taking note of the local flavour combinations, rustic dishes and the sellers' personal and casual connection to their customers. Thankfully for Londoners, he decided to give it a go himself, and such is the demand for his Korean fusion dishes that he now has to make over two kilograms of kimchi a week.

The vegetables O'Sullivan uses are all sourced from local Asian markets and the meat is from his local butcher in Walthamstow, because, he says, their meat is very high quality and he loves the life they bring to the street—a trait he transfers to his own customers, whether on Eat Street, at this summer's Streetfeast or at the in-vogue market on Hackney's Chatsworth Road.

Luardos
Brockley Market
Lewisham College Car Park
Lewisham Way
SE4 1UT
www.brockleymarket.com

Eat St
Kings Boulevard
N1C
www.east.st

Whitecross Street Market
Whitecross Street
EC1Y 8JL

No phone
www.luardos.co.uk

It's hard to miss the vintage Luardos "Mexivans". Luridly painted in hot pink and turquoise—and named "Mary" and "Jesus H Van", respectively—they're a ubiquitous sight on the London street food scene, as well as the summer festival circuit. But given the enduring popularity of the food, paired with the founders' dedication to fresh produce and strictly on-the-day preparation, it is possible to miss the food. Not something you want to happen given the heady acclaim in which their carnitas and slow-cooked beef are held.

Run by Simon Luard, John Bell and Sarah Maxwell, Luardos can be found around town at Eat St, Whitecross Street Market and Brockley Market. Their burritos are popular because of their insistence on simplicity; their use of the freshest ingredients; their crunchy, fresh and fiery homemade salsas; and legendarily generous dollops of guacamole. From time to time they diversify with fish tacos, but the stalwart carnitas—cooked everyday from half a pig, cooking juices from their chorizo, and a special mix of paprika, cumin and cinnamon, roasted until meltingly juicy and tender—are a classic and deserved signature dish. Use of a bib recommended.

THE RED HERRING SMOKE HOUSE

The Red Herring Smoke House
Brockley Market
Lewisham College Car Park
Lewisham Way
SE4 1UT
www.brockleymarket.com

Eat St
Kings Boulevard
N1C
www.eat.st

07567 85569

www.theredherringsmokehouse.com

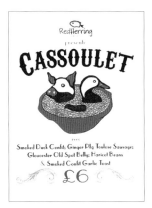

The Red Herring Smoke House is a local London treasure. After building a DIY cold smoker with a friend and initially experimenting with Welsh sea trout, Peter Hogan's enterprise soon diversified to expand their trade to local delis. Street food was the next logical step. At first becoming known for their signature "The Whole Hog"—a smoked Gloucester Old Spot bacon BLT with smoked Keen's cheddar and a fried egg—they've since re-expanded their range with cassoulets, croquettes, a smoked duck confit sandwich and "Smoked Shrimp Po' Boys". Particularly endearing of these is the cassoulet: the one we tasted was deliciously smokey and subtly sweet, made from their smoked confit duck legs and Old Spot bacon, the Ginger Pig's Toulouse sausages and dried haricot beans. The Red Herring Smoke House is now a full-time street-crawling endeavour.

Hogan admits that developing new products—particularly the constituent research and "digging around" that goes into this—is as much of a pull as the technical smoking side of things and the thrill of being part of the burgeoning London street food scene. Appropriately, provenance of ingredients is of high importance. Most meat is sourced form the Rare Breed Meat Company. They also source from a network of small local producers who rear free-range Aylesbury ducks, Hereford and Longhorn cattle and proper free-range chickens. Keen's Cheddar from Somerset also supply their farmhouse butter. The bread used is Campaillou from Jade's Bakery in Blackheath.

THE RIB MAN

The Rib Man
Brick Lane (Sundays)
E1

Eat St
Kings Boulevard
N1C
www.eat.st

No phone
www.theribman.co.uk

The Rib Man knows his stuff. Having been a butcher, Mark Gevaux was already aware of the perfect ways to get the most tender and delicious meat from the rib cut—a notoriously tricky one to cook as effectively as the pit masters of the American deep south. But it is those barbecue kings that the rib man is often compared to—high praise, and validated by anyone who has had one of his large buns stuffed with melting barbecued rib meat pulled from the bone.

Obviously aware he's on to a good thing, Gevaux keeps it simple, serving only the titular fare, which he cooks on site starting at 3am in order that the meat is mouth-wateringly tender by lunchtime. All ribs are baby back from outdoor-reared pigs sourced through Norfolk and Suffolk farms. He serves them simply, too; as either full or half racks, and the aforementioned stripped meat filling his wraps and rolls. What makes them particularly special is that Gevaux also makes all his own sauces, setting him apart from most barbecue street-traders. His smoky barbecue sauce is the perfect combination of sweet and sticky; his hot sauce tellingly fiery. Finally, Gevaux's "Holy Fuck" number, made from scotch bonnets and naga chillies, needs little further explanation.

TONGUE 'N CHEEK

Tongue 'n Cheek
Eat St
Kings Boulevard
N1C
www.eat.st

07414 446545
www.tonguencheek.info

Tongue 'n Cheek does what it says on the tin: ox and pig tongue and cheek, cooked to tender perfection, served in a densely reduced cooking liquid in a sort-of-stew form—see the exquisite "Ox cheek with mushrooms and polenta"—or slapped in a bun. The man behind it, Christiano Meneghin, accurately believes not only that to make good use of underrated meat cuts is positive in its sustainability, but that offal cuts—often seen as unpleasant by the general public—are actually more complex and tasty then the average cuts you'll find on many menus. Tongue 'n Cheek maintains its hip credentials in ethical eating by pushing this awareness of under-used meat and sourcing from local suppliers, with a seasonal bent.

In starting the stall, Meneghin—a passionate Italian keen to share his love of slow-cooked offal dishes—found the perfect vehicle for combining his cultural background with current demand for getting good food fast. He loves reinvigorating the classics he grew up with. For the popular signature "Porky Sub", thin pork cheeks are slowly cooked in a Port reduction until meltingly tender and served in a soft sub roll—American-style, with a spicy slaw. Such dishes are a shining example of what street food does best: amalgamating different cultures and techniques, and delivering unrivalled taste, when and where the customer wants it, and all for only a minimal price point. Success all round.

YUM BUN

Yum Bun
Broadway Market Schoolyard
Westgate Street
E8 3RL
www.broadwaymarket.co.uk

Eat St
Kings Boulevard
NIC
www.eat.st

07919 408221
www.yumbun.co.uk

At Yum Bun you *could* have a micro-feast on vegetarian buns made with miso glazed portabello mushrooms, but to do so would miss the delicious combination that epitomises the sweet-yet-meaty combination so well known in Chinese cookery —*char sui bau*, the steamed pork bun.

Yum Bun make theirs slightly differently to the traditional counterpart. The individual buns are filled more like wraps or sandwiches than the sweet puffed up parcels you might find in Chinatown. Yum Bun's are homemade steamed organic rice flour buns, cut in half and filled with a combination of slow-cooked barbecued pork belly—importantly with its layer of juicy fat intact—both hoisin sauce for sweetness and shriracha for heat, and topped off with crunchy, cool spring onions and cucumber slices. Carefully sourcing their ingredients is an important aspect of the stall's ethos; with the vegetables coming from a nearby Broadway Market stall and the Blythburgh pork from the Rare Meat Co, their provenance is easily traceable.

Lisa Meyer and Jacob Walters started Yum Bun at Broadway Market in September 2010, and it has since become a well-known London street food fixture. Alongside their pork buns they also offer the veggie option and a varying selection of Asian broths which could satisfy even the most health-conscious. Despite this, their pork buns are still undoubtedly the star attraction, with many customers coming back for seconds, thirds, and even—purportedly—a sixth.

BROOKS BUTCHERS

Brooks Butchers
91 Chamberlayne Road
NW10 3ND

020 8964 5678
www.brooksbutchers.com

Self-titled "modern style butchers" Brooks are a recent—and welcome—addition to bustling Kensal Rise; in fact, they are the meat-centric spin off of the award-winning Minkie's deli cafe just across the road. Combining modern and traditional butchery skills with a passion for quality produce, Brooks Butchers guarantee only the best for your table. Produce is selected with animal welfare, breed purity and taste in mind, and the meat sold by Brooks shows a knowing concern for regionality and seasonality.

The butchers are happy to tailor their knowledge and skills to each customer's needs: whether it is dry-aging beef to an exact request—although they do it themselves for a good 42 days—seam butchering or curing meats, you can be sure it will be done expertly. Traditional cuts are the principal attractions, although prepared edibles like their acclaimed homemade sausage rolls are well worth a mention. Standard cuts of meats like chicken, duck, pork, beef and lamb join seasonal game, tasty sausages and organic bacon to satisfy the most exigent clientele. Slow-roast legs of lamb, beef rib eyes, smoked bacon and rotisserie chicken are some shop favourites, although nothing seems to beat the juicy, marbled goodness of their steaks. Pay a visit and see if you can leave the shop empty-handed— some locals seem to be having a bit of trouble with that.

DOVE & SON

Dove & Son
71 Northcote Road
Battersea
SW11 6PJ

020 7223 5191
www.doveandson.co.uk

Bob Dove is a third generation Master Butcher, providing knowing Clapham and Battersea residents with exemplary, well-sourced meat, by way of his striking shop on the yuppyish, brand-riddled Northcote Road. Founded by HG Dove in 1889, the institution still remains on the very same spot it was first based, and many of the original features remain. It is almost 30 years since Bob started sourcing quality British produce for the store. Provenance is key here, with prime beef and lamb from Scotland and North Yorkshire, British farm-derived rare breed pork and free-range poultry, homemade sausages and seasonal varieties of game being a common sight.

As well as butchery, in-house chef—and proprietor of Dove's deli—Jo Hopwood hand-prepares a variety of pies, Szechuan pork belly, roasted gammon, scotch eggs, salads, and even items as unexpected as soups and ice creams.

Service is charmingly gruff, but Bob and his staff are committed to their trade and deservedly praised for the high standard of their fare.

JAMES ELLIOTT

James Elliott
96 Essex Road
N1 8LU

020 7226 3658

The old-fashioned wooden sign and beautifully displayed produce laid out in the front window are a sign of the traditional butcher's experience afforded by James Elliott's shop on Essex Road.

For many, James Elliott is *the* go-to store for excellent quality meat and produce in North London. Free-range poultry and pork, lamb from Lincolnshire and carefully aged Scotch premier beef are all carefully kept and prepared in-house. Of particular note is the shop's extensive range of sausages, including Toulouse style, wild boar and apple, venison and redcurrant, and a spicy lamb merguez. A selection of mustards and English cheeses broaden the culinary spectrum.

Highly knowledgeable and thoroughly committed to their trade, the staff of James Elliott will happily help advise on devising recipes, how to cook different cuts of meat and how to store produce effectively. Many customers profess to leaving the shop better informed than when they went in: always a good sign of a quality establishment.

GINGER PIG

Ginger Pig

Hackney
Lauriston Road
E9 7HJ

020 7871 0461
www.thegingerpig.co.uk

Shepherds Bush
137–139 Askew Road
W12 9AU

020 8740 4297

Marylebone
8–10 Moxon Street
W1U 4EW

020 7935 7788

Waterloo
Greensmiths
27 Lower Marsh
SE1 7RG

020 7921 2975

London Bridge
Borough Market
SE1 1TL

020 7403 4721

"There is no great secret to what we do: we simply raise the best animals, in the happiest of circumstances, on the finest stretch of Yorkshire Moors we could find. Only by ensuring that our pigs, cattle and sheep receive the highest level of care can we be sure our customers will receive the quality they have come to expect. It's not a philosophy or mission statement. It's just what we do."—Tim Wilson, founder.

The Ginger Pig—comprising the aforementioned Yorkshire farms, as well as five stores in London—has come to be lauded as one of the finest butchers in the capital. Known as much for their faultless sausage rolls, pies and scotch eggs as their impeccably sourced and butchered meat, the company has garnered both a casual and critical following, with their produce being publicly praised by Jay Rayner and sourced by the Hawksmoor group for their equally loved London steakhouses. Unlike most other London butchers, Ginger Pig maintains a city-wide presence, with stores in as diversely spread out locations as Hackney, Marylebone, Borough Market, Greensmiths independent supermarket on Waterloo's Lower Marsh and, most recently, Shepherd's Bush.

FRANK GODFREY

Frank Godfrey
7 Highbury Park
N5 1QJ

020 7226 2425
www.godfreys.co

Butchery had long been an established skill in Frank Godfrey's family by the time he founded his first shop in 1905, and the butchers' continuing pursuit of exemplary quality is an apt tribute to this lineage. Frank's great-grandchildren, Jerry, Christopher and Phillip, currently run the long-standing business. Their different areas of expertise make Godfrey's one of the best-regarded butchers in London. They are proud of their "hands-on" approach to butchery, and they regularly visit the supplying farms, checking on the wellbeing, husbandry and pedigree of the animals. It is no surprise that they are one of the founding members of the esteemed Guild of Q Butchers, promoting the highest standards of animal care.

Godfrey's varied fare and commitment in creating a positive experience for the customer has earned them a loyal clientele, which includes prestigious food journalists, writers, and chefs. They also run well-regarded home butchery courses and will train you in dissecting basic cuts and making sausages (apt given that Frank Godfrey's much loved Lincolnshire sausage recipe is still used in the shop today), sending you home with the fruits of your effort, a boning knife and a full stomach.

KEEVIL & KEEVIL

Keevil & Keevil
218 Central Markets
Smithfield
EC1A 9LH

020 7248 3185
www.keevilandkeevil.co.uk

There has been a market at Smithfield for almost a thousand years. The area was a burial site in Roman times and later became a popular location for public executions. Later still the land was a grassy plain and, since the late fourteenth century, the centre of livestock trade outside of the London city walls.

Keevil & Keevil is the oldest butcher in Smithfield. It was the result of four family butchers' merging in 1908, the oldest of them founded in 1794. Their lengthy presence at Smithfield Market has involved firewatching during the Second World War and surviving the great fire of 1958, which destroyed a great part of the market. George Abrahams—a Smithfield trader specialising in imported meats—bought Keevil & Keevil in 1991, developing a focus on more unusual cuts alongside top quality, everyday fare. Their commitment to beef of the highest standards is reflected in their carefully chosen British, Australian, Brazilian and Argentinean suppliers; for instance, Oakleigh Ranch in Eastern Australia provides them with Wagyu beef, derived from the world-famous black Japanese breeds. Traditionally-bred New Zealand lamb, seasonal British game, and more exotic meats such as crocodile tail and kangaroo are other highlights of their vast repertoire. Additionally, Keevil & Keevil pride themselves in being the only London wholesaler of the award-winning Macsween Scottish haggis, available in a range of adaptations, from a popular vegetarian adaptation to cocktail-sized portions.

KENT & SONS

Kent & Sons
59 St John's Wood High Street
NW8 7NL

020 7722 2258
www.kents-butchers.co.uk

Kent & Sons opened in 1919, when Fred Kent moved from Wiltshire to ply his butcher's trade in the capital. He used to operate a string of butchers' shops, though sadly only one remains, at the current St John's Wood location.

As part of the Guild of Q Butchers, they are renowned for their high quality meat, dedication to the British farming industry and ready dispensation of informed advice on butchery. Customers have been quick to praise their excellent Dutch veal and Cornish lamb, but the real draw at Kent's is their Aberdeen Angus beef, which they hang for at least 28 days, imparting a stronger depth of flavour and a melt-in-the-mouth tenderness. Prices aren't cheap, but patrons are guaranteed wonderful produce and consistently high standards of service.

The Kent & Sons website also acts as a useful reference archive, with detailed information on cooking times and how to prepare difficult cuts. For the more cookery-phobic amongst us, they also have a good range of oven-ready meals; their fish pie gets particularly rave reviews. In addition, Kent & Sons runs butchery and sausage-making courses, and participants can take home a goody bag containing edible evidence of their recently acquired skills.

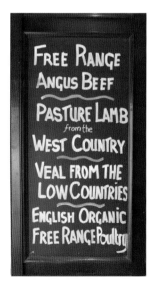

C LIDGATE

C Lidgate
110 Holland Park Avenue
W11 4UA

020 7727 8243
www.lidgates.com

C Lidgate—a five generation family business—is probably the best-known butcher in the UK, let alone London. Established in 1858, the business is over 150 years old and has been consistently popular due to its impeccable standards and excellent fare. Meat is always free from additives, hormones, antibiotics and growth promoters, and is sourced carefully by the current proprietor, Danny Lidgate, and his father. Suppliers include Judith Freane, Highgrove—the home farm of HRH the Prince of Wales—and Gatcombe Park—the home farm of HRH the Princess Royal; all are known for their longstanding organic credentials.

Although their shop on Holland Park Avenue is stuffed full of the best quality raw meats—from sausages (reputedly "the perfect banger") and pork belly, to organic grass-fed beef, game and even ostrich—the butchers also produce cooked pies so delectable that they earned the top spot in England's Best Steak Pie Award. C Lidgate also stocks various pre-cooked snacks and meals, including an infamously good scotch egg. They have received countless awards, including nine Gold Medals at the 2011 Smithfield Awards and many Great Taste Awards; the latter, given by the Guild of Fine Food, are described as the "epicurean equivalent of the Booker Prize".

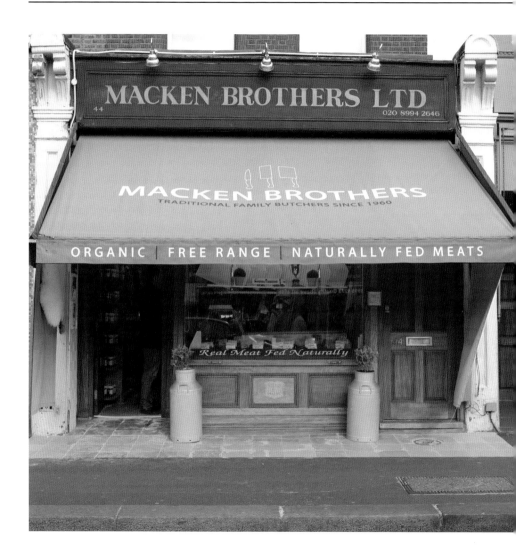

MACKEN BROTHERS

Macken Brothers
44 Turnham Green Terrace
W4 1QP

020 8994 2646
www.mackenbros.co.uk

Serving both the public and the catering trade for over half a century, Macken Brothers was established in 1960 by the Irishmen Jim and Peter Macken. The Chiswick-based family butchers was taken over by brothers Rodney and Jimmy Macken after their parents' retirement, and the business has grown steadily since then.

The shop's reputation relies on the combination of an informal and endearing personal service—described across the board as "helpful and chatty"—and a staunch dedication to the sourcing of high quality, naturally-fed meats from England, Wales, Scotland and Ireland. On top of typical butchers' fare—Aberdeen Angus beef, seasonal lamb from Shetland and Wales, Gloucester Old Spot pork, sausages made with their own special recipes, and renowned poultry breeds—they also supply game and more exotic meats, such as buffalo, ostrich and kudu upon request.

Macken Brothers is one to visit for a cut of meat beyond the quality you'll find in most supermarkets and butchers. They'll also happily dish out idiosyncratic, homespun advice on recipes; a shoulder of lamb is cooked, they will tell you, when "the whole house smells of it". Their already-impressive career has recently seen them take the prestigious position of running their own meat counter in the Oxford Street branch of Selfridges.

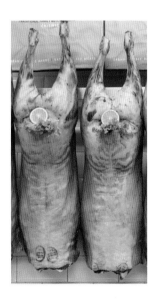

MEAT N16

Meat N16
104 Stoke Newington
Church Street
N16 0LA

020 7254 0724
www.meatlondon.co.uk

Meat N16 is a new gem in Stoke Newington Church Street's collection of independent businesses, which fall between the achingly trendy and the family-friendly. Opened by Paul Grout—former butchery and charcuterie manager at Harvey Nichols—and wine merchant Marc Wise—of Planet of the Grapes—Meat N16 is causing a stir amongst both locals and foodie pilgrims alike. Their success derives from a combination of a clean, modern aesthetic and a devotion to free-range meat of the highest quality.

The staff at Meat N16 pride themselves on their respect for animal welfare and traditional farming lore. Their beef comes from the Aberdeen Angus breed of cattle; the meat is visibly hung for at least 20 days before being cut to the customer's preference. They also source Dorset Down sheep, known as the "king of the prime lamb breed", which are ideal for organic breeding. Their pork is all free-range, and their bacon and sausages are made on-site. Free-roaming Packington chickens and carefully sourced feathered and furred game complete the meaty picture, whilst homemade marinades and pungent cheeses are also readily available.

Monthly courses are offered on subjects such as sausage making and lamb cutting, which take place at their open-plan store. The cherry on the top of Meat N16's impressive set-up is its generous wine cellar and wine-tasting room, with bottles sorted by the cuts of meat that they best compliment. They'll sharpen your knives too!

MILLER OF KENSINGTON

Miller of Kensington
14 Stratford Road
W8 6QD

020 7937 1777

If the enormous collection of model frogs in the window doesn't entice you enough, the meat at Miller of Kensington will. The butcher's was founded over 65 years ago, and has been managed for the last 25 by Mohamed el Banna. Under his tutelage, the shop provides its broad clientele—whether Kensington locals or in-the-know individuals from further afield—with produce from the best sources in Britain.

Miller's veal is particularly well regarded, though its lamb and poultry are also widely acclaimed, and are available both in organic and halal varieties. All products, whether unpasteurised milk or Japanese beef, are sourced through local London markets such as Smithfield. Meat is also sold pre-cooked and available through the shop's catering service for larger functions, such as birthdays, weddings, Thanksgivings and Christmas dinners. Their popular cooked turkey delivery is intended for those who might want to skip the kitchen legwork and devote their time to other less-stressful festive activities.

One should expect an idiosyncratically singular customer service at Miller; though there may be a timetable on the board outside, it is also made clear that the shop's lunch break will take place when the butcher is hungry. But when the product sold is this decent, who are we to complain? If you are looking to diversify a little from meat, Miller of Kensington also has a Mediterranean and French food store a just a short distance the road.

M MOEN & SONS

M Moen & Sons
24 The Pavement
Clapham Common
SW4 0JA

020 7622 1624
www.moen.co.uk

Garry Moen's M Moen & Sons is a butcher's at heart, but it offers such a wide range of products that it has rightly been called a farmers' market in its own right. Now perched on the edge of Clapham Common, the shop has moved location a couple of times since Maurice Moen founded it in 1971. The service, however, has not changed a bit, and is enhanced by the beautiful shop architecture, which was restored to its original Victorian state with the help of grants from English Heritage and the National Lottery.

Organic, free-range meat from carefully vetted suppliers comes in an astonishing variety: besides beef, lamb, pork and poultry, Moen's offers seasonal game such as pheasant and wild duck, homemade sausages, prepared stir-fries, marinated and stuffed lamb, and veal meatballs. Moen's either stock or will happily order seasonal goods such as Burns night haggis and Christmas geese, and any offal you might desire. If you find yourself short on recipe ideas, the pile of cookbooks by the counter will help inspire you.

Expert butchery is only the beginning of M Moen & Sons' remit: cured hams, pâtés, smoked salmon, French charcuterie, artisan bread, selected cheeses, jams, fresh vegetables, a mouth-watering selection of prepared olives, and many more treats from specialist suppliers cover the counters. On a weekend morning, you might want to let the scent guide you towards the shop; the skewer-roasted pork sandwiches on offer will make your day.

WILLIAM ROSE

William Rose
126 Lordship Lane
East Dulwich
SE22 8HD

020 8693 9191
www.williamrosebutchers.com

75 East Dulwich Grove
East Dulwich
SE22 8PR

020 8693 7733

The all-day Saturday queues on Lordship Lane outside William Rose butchers are a decent indication of the quality of the fare sold within. Established in Vauxhall in 1862, this family business moved to East Dulwich in 2005. The opening of a second branch—on nearby East Dulwich Grove—is testament to the good practises of the shop, as well as an increasing local demand for good produce. Unsurprisingly, they are one of the finest butchers in South East London.

The shop stocks seasonal rare breeds such as Longhorn, Sussex, Devon and Welsh Black beef. Other highlights include Jimmy Butler's award-winning Blythburgh free-range pork, wild venison from Balmoral and Royal Deeside in the Cairngorn uplands, and their celebrated range of homemade sausages, including a Gloucester Old Spot breakfast variety and gluten-free lamb sausages.

William Rose also actively encourage the good old-fashioned bond between butcher and patron; heated discussions between members of staff about which cut of beef would be best for a particular roast are not unheard of. It isn't a surprise that their Carnivore Club—a tutorial for customers who would like to improve their skills with the knife—is extremely popular and fully booked well in advance. William Rose believe that knowledge should be passed on for the benefit of everyone, and they regularly take on apprentices keen to adopt the traditional skills of the butcher.

TRADITIONAL BUTCHERS, EST 1952
ORGANIC SINCE 1989

GG SPARKES

GG Sparks
24 Old Dover Road
SE3 7BT

020 8355 8597

North Cross Road Market
East Dulwich
SE22

Known for the quality and reliability of their meat, GG Sparkes' loyal customers in South East London are prepared to travel—and wait—for the butcher's excellent produce. Queues are particularly long on Saturdays at the flagship Blackheath store, but this is relieved by the recent addition of a mobile unit, affectionately known as the "meat van", serving customers at North Cross Road market in East Dulwich.

Sparkes is an exceptionally helpful butcher, the kind of man who will patiently answer questions about cooking, advise on ingredients and go the extra mile for a visitor to the shop. There are even reports of him throwing in cuts of meat for free because he is sure that they will improve the stew a customer is intending to cook. The shop's homemade cracked pepper sausages are lauded amongst his regulars, as is his cheery demeanour. And if you can't face leaving the house, the shop will deliver.

GG Sparkes was established in 1952 and has been the receiver of constant plaudits since. They are listed as one of Rick Stein's London Food Heroes for their commitment to organic meat and free-range poultry—including the feted Label Anglais breed—and their policy of paying farmers a fair price, helping to promote a sustainable rural economy.

HG WALTER

HG Walter
51 Palliser Road
W14 9EB

020 7385 6466
www.hgwalter.com

Peter Heanen founded HG Walter in 1972. Since then, the Barons Court-based family business has regularly been voted the best small butcher's shop in Great Britain and the best butcher in London and the Southeast. Aside from the superb quality of their organic and free-range meat, it is the wide variety of their produce, excellent credentials and willingness to dispense knowledgeable advice that makes them many Londoners' favourite butcher. Customers are encouraged to ask Walter's Leiths-trained Head Chef how to cook their Aberdeen Angus beef—hung for at least 28 days—their seasonal lamb, their tender veal and their pork, supplied by free-range pig farmer Hugh Norris. Show particular interest in their practice and they might even offer you a seat to observe from whilst preparing your T-bone.

The shop's award-winning prepared meats are made of top quality raw materials: their teriyaki sirloin, lamb burger with mango, ginger and fresh mint, and Walter's oriental ribs marinated in hoi sin sauce are an example of the tasty goods that await the more adventurous. For extra culinary kudos, their sausages are a firm favourite of chefs such as Heston Blumenthal and Claude Bosi.

HG Walter's savoury pies have won gold in the Great Taste Awards several times, and the wide array of selected cheeses, sauces, pickles, pastas and even organic vegetables make a visit to Barons Court a worthwhile one.

THANKS

At Black Dog Publishing, thanks must first go to Leonardo Collina, whose expert design and excellent photography have totally made the book. Editorially, many thanks to Arrate Hidalgo, Prudence Ivey and Phoebe Stubbs for their invaluable assistance with writing and research.

Thanks to: Thomas Blythe, Abiye Cole, Alex Sergeant, Alix Leonard, Rob Shaw, Jonathon Jones, Aysegul Dirik, Ben Campbell, Ben Denner, Max, Owen and Salvatore at Brawn, Cooper Deville, John Rattagan, Sarah and Ollie at The Bull & Last, Candice Hawthorne, Fergus Henderson, Trevor Gulliver, Charlotte Allen, Chloe Hannah, Louise at Hix Oyster & Chop House, Kimberley Brown, Chris Godfrey, Claire Strickett, Christiano Meneghin, Daniel O'Sullivan, Danny Lidgate, Bob Dove, Garry Moen, David Harrison, Debora Luiz, Fiona St George, Penny Watson, David Eyre, Steve at Eyre Brothers, Frank Boxer, Geeti Singh, Gemma McAloon, Tom Pemberton, Clare Heanen, Hugh Fowler, Ian Hutchison, Irena Pogarcic, Jackie McDevitt, Tim Hayward, Jez Felwick, Joel Henderson, Lisa Meyer, Petra Barran, Francesca at Deli West One, Kevin Rackind, Lucy Hayward, Luke Bishop, Mark Jankel, Mel Papa, Mark Gevaux, Melanie Arnold, Rosminah Brown, Natalie Raw, Natasha Polak, Nathan Mills, Brett Perkins, Peter Hogan, Pilar Garcia, Simon at Pitt Cue Co., Richard Jocelyn, Ricky McMenemy, Rodney Franklin, Tim Sheehan, Roger Faulks, Simon Luard, Simon Mullins, Sophie Boden, Toby Allen, Tom Oldroyd, Michael at The Eagle, Bruno Loubet, Lewis Hannaford, Margot Henderson, Melanie Arnold, Tom Barton, Stefan Schafer, Paul Winch-Furness, Johnnie Pakington, Scott Grummett, Kaya Toyoshima.

AUTHOR BIO

Thomas Blythe was general manager and maître d' at Fergus Henderson's St John restaurant for more than a decade. Thomas is now a freelance consultant and writer contributing to among others GQ.com, *Port Magazine* online, *Observer Food Monthly* and the food quarterly *Fire & Knives*.

Black Dog Publishing Limited
10A Acton Street
London
WC1X 9NG

t.   +44 (0)207 713 5097
f.   +44 (0)207 713 8682
e.   info@blackdogonline.com
www.blackdogonline.com

Edited at Black Dog Publishing by Thomas Howells

Designed at Black Dog Publishing by Leonardo Collina

ISBN 978 1 907317 88 0

Black Dog Publishing is an environmentally responsible company.
Meat London: An Insider's Guide is printed on FSC accredited paper.

Also available:
A Guide to London's Classic Cafes and Fish & Chip Shops
Tea & Cake London

art design fashion
history photography
theory and things

www.blackdogonline.com